THEATRE POSTERS

THEATRE POSTERS

Aileen Reid

MAGNA
BOOKS

Published by Magna Books
Magna Road
Wigston
Leicester LE18 4ZH

Produced by Bison Books Ltd
Kimbolton House
117A Fulham Road
London SW3 6RL

ISBN 1-85422-417-4

Printed in Spain

Contents and List of Plates

Introduction

Despite their appeal, both to those interested in the graphic arts and to theatre enthusiasts, the literature on theatre posters in scanty. Most works concentrate on posters in general or on the theater in general. The problems of studying the art form are compounded by the peculiar ephemerality of theatre posters. More than almost any other kind of poster the theatre poster's life is limited to a few weeks, that is to a single run, sometimes even a single performance, of a play. This is a pity as theatre posters have a pivotal role to play in the histories of two important art forms, and the increasing status of the theatre as a form of entertainment, especially in the last hundred years,

has enticed some of the greatest artists to design theatre posters.

The history of theatre posters is of course directly related to that of the theatre but it by no means mirrors it. While a form of theatre that we can recognize was established in Athens by the sixth century BC, most of the posters in this book date from the nineteenth and twentieth centuries. This difference is partly a consequence of the way that theatre organization and management has changed over the centuries. But of perhaps greater importance are the great developments in printing techniques, and even in paper production, which have occured ever since printing was first de-

veloped at the end of the fifteenth century.

In Classical Greece all free men had access to the theatre and it enjoyed a veneration comparable to that accorded the games at Olympia. No evidence of publicity of any kind survives and it is likely that it would have been unnecessary given the status of the theatre as part political institution and part shrine. The theatre in Classical Rome was, as befits a more diverse and pragmatic society, more concerned with entertainment on a grand scale. Excavations at Pompeii have revealed a variety of political and economic propaganda which suggests that theatrical publicity probably existed, both for

Below left: The theatre in Classical Greece enjoyed the status almost of a political institution but no promotional material of any kind is known to survive.

Below: Seventeenth-century traveling players.

Below: The Globe Theatre in Southwark, south London, famed for presentations of Shakespeare's plays.

large-scale serious drama and for smaller, more rustic productions by itinerant players; unfortunately none survives.

In the middle ages the theatre was largely controlled by the church and its purpose was thus to encourage the populace through the medium of mystery, miracle, nativity and Passion plays, to devote themselves to God and the church. The projected audience was largely illiterate and the purpose of the venture was not profit, at least not in the monetary sense, which suggests that publicity material was not a major concern. Nonetheless a handwritten theatre bill for a Passion play in Hamburg in 1466 has survived which suggests that the practice was not unusual.

With the loosening of church control throughout the sixteenth and seventeenth centuries came a huge proliferation in secular drama, both high theatre spectacular for the upper echelons of society, and various forms of entertainment and street threatre aimed at the masses. In the earlier

part of this period performances were generally announced by a spectacularly noisy parade through the streets by the performers, but as time progressed and literacy spread, playbills assumed an increasing importance. These were usually small, letterpress sheets which served the dual purpose of indicating the date and place of performance and, like a modern theatre program, listing the members of the cast.

Two important developments in the emergence of the modern theatre posters took place at the end of the eighteenth century. One was the introduction of commercial advertising on playbills. Concerns such as restaurants and fashion houses paid for the printing costs of playbills in exchange for advertising space. This led to the development of substantial theatre programs largely made up of advertising for which the audience was expected to pay. This is one reason that the promotional and program functions of playbills diversified into separate programs and posters.

The other significant development for poster art in general was the invention in 1798 of lithography by Aloys Senefelder. Since the mid-eighteenth century some theatre posters, especially in France, had been illustrated, first with woodcuts later with steel engravings. Letterpress remained, however, the norm for theatre posters as these methods of illustration were uneconomically expensive, especially when several colors were used. Lithography, which in the early days involved drawing the design in wax or oil on stone and which relied on the principle of oil repelling water, allowed multicolored, large-size images to be produced relatively cheaply.

This development coincided with an explosion in advertising. Without controls posters of all kinds were plastered on

walls, or wherever there was a space, covering anything that happened to be there already. Bill-poster became a common working-class occupation, while others were 'sandwich men,' a form of advertising still occasionally seen today. Partly in order to limit the indiscriminate display of posters, by the mid-nineteenth century specially built advertising hoardings or billboards, and, especially in France, pillars were being erected.

The net result of this sudden proliferation of posters was that the artistic merit of many posters was not high. A milestone in the emergence of the theatre poster as art came in 1871 with the Olympic Theatre, London's poster for a dramatization of Wilkie Collins's *The Woman in White*. This poster is significant for several reasons. It is striking for the minimal amount of information included, with only the title of the play and the name of the theatre. The curiosity which this excites is enhanced by the artistic impact of the image of the woman. An almost abstract pattern of swirls in the

woman's cloak is made all the more startling as it is rendered purely in black and white.

The poster is from a woodcut by W H Hooper working from a drawing of Frederick Walker's and several aspects of their collaboration reflect contemporary artistic tastes and trends. At this period Japanese prints were collected and studied by artists and people of 'taste', and theatre advertising had a long history in Japanese printmaking. Significantly too, Japanese prints are produced by woodcut with the artist supplying a drawing which is translated into a print by, successively, a blockcutter and a printer. This collaborative approach was enjoying a revival in the west at this time as a symptom of the arts and crafts movement one of whose tenets was the equal value of the fine and decorative, including graphic, arts. Certainly Walker believed that posters had specific design criteria which made them an artform in themselves; his *Woman in White* poster exemplifies this belief and paved the way for the great poster artists of the Belle Epoque, preeminent among whom were Jules Chéret and Henri de Toulouse-Lautrec.

Jules Chéret was firstly a lithographer and only secondly an artist. He spent some time in England and although he

MR GARRICK in BENEDICT
in Much ado about nothing.

9

such as the Moulin Rouge and the Moulin de la Galette. Proprietors of these establishments vied with each other using among other marketing techniques, ever larger, more exotic and more 'artistic' posters.

Many artists were attracted by this demi-monde of the café-concert and music hall. Some, such as Henri de Toulouse-Lautrec, designed posters, while an artist such as Chéret, although not trained as a painter, clearly shows in his posters the influence of contemporary Impressionist painting. Chéret's mastery of his medium enabled him to reproduce subtle effects of lights and reflexion or, if the occasion demanded, the boldness of simple shapes and outlines which are the more usual characteristics of print-making.

Perhaps the prime example of Chéret's skill is one of the posters he produced to advertise the American dancer Loïe Fuller when she was doing a show at the Folies-Bergère in 1893. Fuller caused a sensation on both sides of the Atlantic with her Serpentine and Fire Dances in which, draped in a billowing diaphanous costume she twirled like a dervish. Changing, colored lights enhanced the effect of tongues of colored flame. Chéret like many of his contemporaries was enchanted by this spectacle and perhaps more than any other artist, even Toulouse-Lautrec, his poster seems to capture the spirit of Loïe Fuller's dancing.

may well have been impressed by the artistic breakthrough which Walker's poster represented he was principally struck by the technical advancement of British printers. British lithographers had developed techniques for printing on much larger sheets of paper than their European contemporaries which of course lent itself ideally to the production of posters. When Chéret returned to Paris he set up his own press. What was unusual for the period was that Chéret both designed and executed his own posters, a practice which distinguished him both from Walker and from the Japanese printmakers they both admired.

Late nineteenth-century Paris was a very fruitful arena for the French theatre. The city's great expansion in the middle years of the century and the creation of Haussmann's Grands Boulevards brought new glamour to the city and large numbers of new working- and middle-class Parisians. Partly as a consequence of this there was a renewed vigor and variety in the theatre. These included established forms of entertainment such as grand opera and the classical theatre of Molière and Racine, as well as prominent contemporary playwrights chief among whom were Augier, Dumas, and Sardou. But there were also new forms of entertainment such as the Opéra Comique and, perhaps more importantly for the history of theatre posters, the café-concert which saw an unprecedented mixing of the classes in the audience, and music halls

Henri de Toulouse-Lautrec's posters are the most famous theatre posters ever produced. His contribution to the medium is also distinctive in that he was the first fine artist who regarded his work as a poster designer as equal to his work as a painter and printmaker; he regarded them as inseparable parts of his artistic oeuvre. As such his approach epitomises the theory which held sway in the late nineteenth century that all the arts, whether fine, decorative, or graphic, were equally important.

Toulouse-Lautrec was uniquely well placed to depict the theatre and music hall and the Parisian demi-monde in general. He took to frequenting the Moulin Rouge, a Montmartre nightclub where the infamous can-can was born, and he lived for a while in a brothel. Wherever he went he sketched the dancers and prostitutes and their clients and audiences, and these formed the basis for his art, in paintings and prints, and, of course, for the posters which advertised these venues.

One reason for the fame and continuing popularity of the nearly forty posters which Toulouse-Lautrec produced are that they have remained startling, both artistically and in their honesty. The main influence on Lautrec's conception of his art, including posters, were the Japanese prints which had become increasingly popular in Britain and France since the opening up of Japan to the west in the mid-1850s. Their influence on Lautrec was twofold. Most obviously, Japanese artists regarded actors and actresses and the theatre in general as a highly acceptable subject for their prints, and this was certainly one stimulus to Lautrec's interest in the theatre.

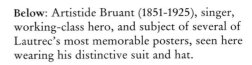

But it was artistic qualities, in particular the spatial organization of Japanese prints which was the salient influence on Lautrec's conception of his posters. Most obviously, of course, was Lautrec's adoption of a strong black outline and areas of unmodulated, bright colors. In Japanese prints these are a natural consequence of their being made up from several different woodblocks, but Lautrec's use of black outline and bright colors is an artistic choice not a technical necessity, given that his posters are lithographs which, as we can see from Chéret's work, is a medium capable of producing subtle color variation.

In Japan there was no tradition of linear perspective as had evolved in the west since the fifteenth century and this liberated artists from certain formal conventions. In particular Japanese artists used devices such as cutting off elements at the edge of the picture and allowing the eye to leap directly from foreground to background. Devices such as these were startling to western eyes in Japanese prints and were all the more so when employed by a French artist such as Lautrec depicting the French theatre. They were almost as shocking as the extent to which Lautrec did not idealize the actors, actresses, and members of the audience he depicted. Such theatrical caricature had, of course, a long history, Honoré Daumier being a prime example earlier in the nineteenth century; what was unprecedented about Lautrec was that he used such unflattering portraits in the very posters which promoted these artists.

Lautrec's vivid characterizations mean that long-dead stars of the Parisian music halls and night clubs, such as May Belfort, La Goulue, Yvette Guilbert, Jane Avril, and Aristide Bruant, are familiar today. Famous actors and actresses had appeared on theatre posters before but usually as ciphers or stereotypes of the pretty leading lady or handsome, virile actor. Lautrec's approach was novel because he sought to capture the individual characteristics of his subject: he is said to have watched Yvette Guilbert thirty times in performance before he successfully captured her likeness. But even more radically he did not necessarily make the show's star the central feature of his poster design. A case in point is his poster for *Le Divan Japonais* where the star Yvette Guilbert is a distant figure on the stage, her head cut off by the top edge of the poster. The center of the poster is

CROQUIS MUSICAUX 17

L'orchestre pendant qu'on joue une tragédie.

Lautrec's social critique in his work in the music halls, night clubs, and cabarets of Montmartre is in spirit akin to the rather uncritical realism of the Goncourt brothers' novels. Théodore Steinlen, on the other hand, was a genuine socialist who sought in the rather unlikely medium of his posters to project some of the more penetrating social commentary of Emile Zola. His poster for a dramatization of Zola's *L'Assommoir* is subdued in tone and artistically and its message is closely related to the café paintings of Edouard Manet of twenty or thirty years earlier. But Steinlen is best known today for his striking poster for Rodolphe Salis' Montmartre cabaret *Le Chat Noir* (page 40), which, in its integration of text and image, shows the artistic debt he owed to Toulouse-Lautrec.

One poster artist who developed the cult of the stage star to an extreme quite different from Lautrec and, especially Steinlen, was Alphonse Mucha. Mucha was an unknown young artist originally from Bohemia when he was discovered by Sarah Bernhardt. She had been dissatisfied by a poster designed by the well-known poster artist Eugène Grasset for a production of *Jeanne Darc* (left). She felt it made her seem insufficiently young and heroic. When she saw Mucha's work she felt he was just the artist to promote her image best; and so it proved. Mucha developed a style of soft, luxuriant colors, sinuous lines, and exotic embellishments of plants and flowers intertwining with flowing locks which epitomize continental Art Nouveau. In his posters for Bernhardt in such productions as *La Dame*

taken up with two members of the audience who are in fact Guilbert's rival Jane Avril and her admirer Edouard Dujardin. Guilbert objected strongly to this apparently demeaning treatment but soon came to recognize the value of Lautrec's work and signed a hundred copies of his poster.

The figure whose name remains most widely known from Lautrec's posters is the actor-manager Aristide Bruant. Bruant was a singer and monologuist who liked to be known as the 'tribune of the people' for the anti-establishment, anti-élitist tone of his delivery. He wore a broad-brimmed felt hat and red scarf and Lautrec concentrated on these attributes and Bruant's physical bulk to suggest very vividly those qualities noted by contemporary commentators. But the most notable feature of the Bruant posters is the extent to which the lettering is a part of the design. With many other theatre-poster designers the lettering was of little consideration, a necessary evil which could only detract from the artistic merits of the design. Even with Chéret's posters, where the lettering has been designed, the poster was usually conceived (and the first proofs produced) without the lettering. Lautrec's designing the lettering as an integral part of the poster, using hand-drawn lines in the manner of the rest of the poster, served more firmly perhaps than any other single development to establish poster design as a distinct branch of art.

aux Camélias and *Gismonda* the tall figure of Bernhardt dominates; often his posters for her had only her name and, perhaps, the title of the play, with all other extraneous lettering excluded thus promoting the cult of La Divine Sarah. Such veneration was a long way from the caricature of Lautrec or the social commentary of Steinlen, and it did not become typical for theatre posters. Perhaps the only near equivalent were film posters for stars such as Garbo in Hollywood's golden age of the 1930s.

To be aware solely of the work of Lautrec, Steinlen, and Mucha is to receive a false impression of the state of French poster art in the late nineteenth and early twentieth century. Although many poster artists took up the most obvious innovations of Lautrec and Chéret, they appeared in a diluted form and much of the impact was lost. Grasset's poster for *Jeanne Darc*, with its conventional figure style and heavy typography was probably more typical of French poster art at this time than anything by Lautrec. This state of affairs was compounded by a downturn in the fortunes of the French theater after 1900. Nonetheless some historically interesting developments did occur such as the 'moral' poster series commissioned from the eminent painter Pierre Puvis de Chavannes in an effort to countermand the supposedly deleterious effects of the 'immoral' posters for the cabarets of Montmartre.

An artistic upturn is not evident until after 1909 when Sergei Diaghilev's Ballets Russes began coming to Paris as part of the Saisons Russes of Russian painting, music, and ballet. Diaghilev valued the designers of his performances as highly as the artistes, and stage sets and costumes were designed by Léon Bakst, Alexander Benois, and Alexander Golovin. In this spirit the Ballets Russes were promoted by posters designed by Jean Cocteau (page 89) and Pablo Picasso in France and Ludwig Kainer in Germany.

It would be a mistake to suppose that artistic theatre posters flourished only in France at the turn of the century. After a period when theatre posters continued to be designed much as they had been in the previous twenty years in England, the challenge thrown out by Walker's *Woman in White* poster was taken up in the 1890s by Aubrey Beardsley. In common with many of his French contemporaries and friends in England such as James Abbott McNeil Whistler, Beardsley studied and admired Japanese art, especially woodblock prints. His main area of work was book and periodical illustration, and his startling use of contrasting black and white was partly derived from his study of Japanese prints. Only rarely did Beardsley venture into color, as he claimed not to have a great feeling for color.

What feeling Beardsley did have for colour he likened to the flat planes of color found in Japanese prints, and this quality characterizes his poster (page 55) for the Avenue Theatre, London's production of John Todhunter's *A Comedy of Sighs* and W B Yeats's *The Land of Heart's Desire*. The female figure has a startling simplicity and her pose is suggestive of the Japanese actor prints popular in the west at the time; another oriental allusion is the rather kitsch 'Japanese' lettering of the theatre's name. Moreover Beardsley's design serves principally as a frame for the text panel; it is thus not markedly different from his other types of graphic work and does not really participate fully in theatre posters as a distinct art form, as Lautrec had done.

The prime example of theatre poster as art in London at this time are the posters produced by James Pryde and William Nicholson who collaborated under the name of the Beggarstaff Brothers. Their first poster was of the actor, later theatre designer, Gordon Craig in the role of Hamlet. Like all their few posters it relies for its effect on a few but exquisitely balanced, simple elements. Each of the Hamlet posters was produced by hand, a labor-intensive method which meant their work was never to be commercially viable. A similar approach to the Hamlet poster was adopted for posters for productions starring Henry Irving, including Becket.

One of the Beggarstaff Brothers' most arresting and perhaps artistically most successful posters was for a production of *Cinderella* at Drury Lane. The vast poster (pages 56-57) was six feet high and nine feet wide; nonetheless the theatre was reputedly dissatisfied with the poster and commissioned the prolific Dudley Hardy to design a replacement. But the truth was that the Beggarstaff Brothers did not like to compromise their artistic integrity for the whims of theatre producers, and the medium of theatre posters demands this. Emblematic of this attitude is their poster of 1895 for the musical *A Trip to Chinatown* (page 58). The central figure is a typical Beggarstaff Brothers design, the figure simply a cut out from the background, the only details being the hair and shoes. So particular were they to get the design 'right' that they pasted on a green square of paper to the righthand corner of every copy of the poster in order to balance the design. The fussy 'oriental' lettering was imposed on the artists by the management and according to a contemporary the Brothers included a note with copies sold to collectors disowning that aspect of the poster.

Perhaps not surprisingly the Beggarstaff Brothers careers as poster designers was short-lived, although Pryde and especially Nicholson had successful careers as painters and printmakers. What the medium demanded was a much more pragmatic approach, especially with regard to cost. Two designers whose enduring success attests to their acceptance of this fact are Dudley Hardy and John Hassall. Hassall went on to design some of the most popular and still-familiar advertising posters, including Andrews' Liver Salts 'I must have left it behind,' but his first foray into the poster genre was as a designer of theater posters, especially

for light entertainment. His popularity rested on his mastery of a robust, accessible humor in his posters which were designed with the importance of the lettering's clarity always in mind.

An artist who enjoyed a success almost equal to Hassall's was Dudley Hardy. He is, perhaps, more interesting from an art-historical point of view in that his work reveals both his indebtedness to developments on the continent and his chameleon-like ability to design in markedly differing styles. His poster for the musical

A Gaiety Girl (page 51) is clearly reminiscent in the lettering and the way the girl is drawn of Chéret's posters in contemporary Paris, yet it lacks the evanescent color of Chéret's work and has a light-hearted solidity akin to Hassall's designs.

Quite a different type of design is his poster for Gilbert and Sullivan's *The Yeoman of the Guard* the first version of which appeared in 1889 (page 50). A much more spartan approach pervades the whole design from the lettering to the drawing of the figure which lacks the calligraphic flourishes which animate *A Gaiety Girl*. Theatre posters after the turn of the century in Britain suffered something of the same withering of quality seen in France, with low-cost mediocre designs, watered-down versions of the popular designs of the 1890s, being mass-produced. It was not until the 1920s that the art was rejuvenated.

Other areas of the world enjoyed a lesser boom in *fin-de-siècle* theatre poster design. In the United States mid-nineteenth century conventions on theatre-poster design prevailed quite late into the century. Even if named actors and actresses were portrayed they were usually presented in a conventionalized form, and designs were often influenced by mass-produced 'cheap and cheerful' circus posters printed in vast numbers by such companies as the Strobridge Company in Cincinnati (pages 28-29). Technical standards were, however, high and 'name' designers such as Matt Morgan, Frederick Scotson-Clark, and Archie Gunn all worked in the US. One of the first native-born American designers to have an impact on poster design was Will Bradley. He was a great admirer of and was strongly influenced by Aubrey Beardsley and like Beardsley he studied Japanese prints. His posters often rely on the manipulation of areas of black and white, but his shapes are simpler than Beardsley's. Many of his designs are closer to the Beggarstaff Brothers in the judicious use of areas of pure color and in the strong and simple typography.

In Berlin, as in France and elsewhere, it was light entertainment and cabaret which produced the first and best artistic theater posters, rather than the 'legitimate' theatre which persisted with restrained, generally typographic, playbills to promote itself. Among the first art-posters were those by Edmund Edel for the American dance-troupe, the Barrison sisters at the Berlin Wintergarten. The success of such posters won commissions

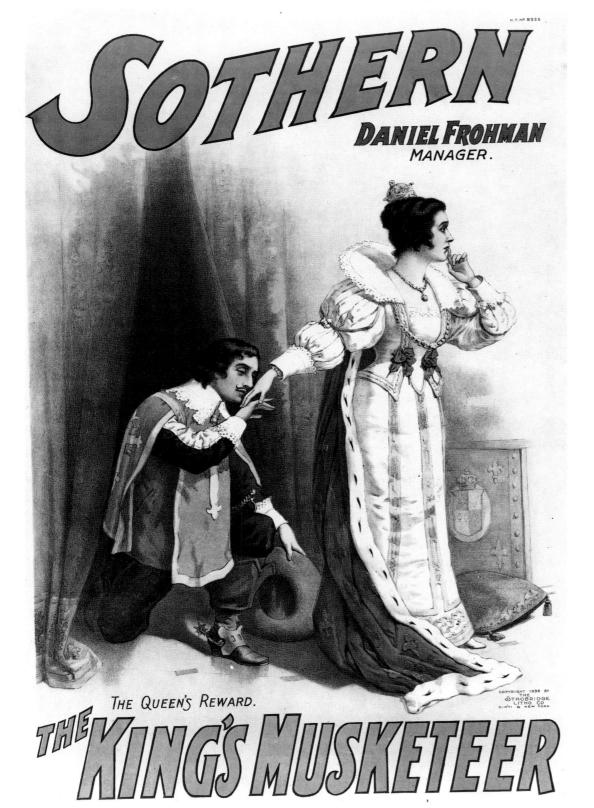

SOTHERN
DANIEL FROHMAN
MANAGER.

THE QUEEN'S REWARD.
THE KING'S MUSKETEER

Below: Oskar Kokoschka (1886-1980) was one of the first 'total' designers producing the set and costume designs as well as the posters for productions, some of which were of his own plays.

Below right: The Czech printmaker Emil Orlik, who designed a number of theatre posters, was unusual in having studied printmaking in Japan.

for Edel for serious drama, including Ibsen's *Love's Comedy* at the Secessionsbuhne in 1899 and Wedekind's *Spring Awakes* in 1903 (page 66).

More important from an artistic viewpoint is the work in Vienna of Emil Orlik. Like Chéret, Orlik preferred to work directly on the lithographic stone himself, and his posters have the directness and integrity of the printmaker's craft. But beyond that, one of his posters in particular came to have a political significance in much the same way, but to much greater extent than Steinlen's *L'Assommoir* poster had. This was his 1897 poster for Gerhart Hauptmann's play *The Weavers*, and his image of workers' suffering, although it may not have been his major intention was read as a statement of solidarity with the many oppressed workers of the Austro-Hungarian Empire. As such it was an important precedent for the campaigning posters of the 1920s. In the years just before World War I a new development took place in theatre-poster design whereby a particular artiste was generally portrayed by a particular designer. Paul Haase made a speciality of portraying in caricature many of the popular stars such as Paul Beckers and Otto Reutter.

While London and, especially, Paris dominated artistic theatre-poster production in the 1890s and Berlin held sway in the following decade, other centers in Europe saw interesting developments despite the relative impoverishment of the theatrical scene compared to the great metropoles. In Hungary Mihaly Biro and Karol Frycz used posters as a means of expressing political messages while in Czechoslovakia artists such as Otokar Stafl and Ludek Marold invested their designs

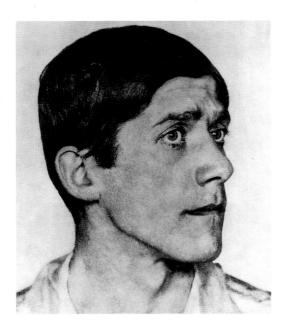

with motifs which expressed their sense of national identity.

An important landmark in theater-poster design was Oskar Kokoschka's 1908 poster for his own play *Murder, Hope of Woman*. Like Lautrec Kokoschka succeeded in integrating the typographic and representational aspects of his poster, an achievement all the more significant as he was principally a painter. The entire production was highly avant-garde, a significant contribution in the development of the Expressionist Movement, and unprecedentedly under the control of one man. The play which treats in a serious manner the conflict of the sexes was written, directed, and the scenes, costumes, and make-up all designed by Kokoschka; the bodies of the actors were painted with bright stripes and blotches and lighting effects, mime, and dramatic gestures all contributed to the dramatic intensity of the play, qual-

ities which are immediately evident in the poster and in other theatre posters he produced at this time (page 67).

One European country which defies the general rules governing theatre in the rest of Europe was Switzerland. With its long history of independence and political isolationism Switzerland was relatively underdeveloped as a center of drama before World War I and its theatre posters reflect this in their rusticity. The outbreak of war in 1914 saw the country swing from provincial backwardness to being a center of international importance as theatre companies flocked to this neutral country from a war-torn Europe. One such was the Deutsches Theater under the legendary Max Reinhardt.

Swiss poster artists, in particular Otto Baumberger (page 75), responded with aplomb to the opportunity provided by working for the cream of European theatrical companies. His poster for

Aeschylus' *Oresteia* is almost equal to Kokoschka's in the expressive intensity of the avenging Orestes who has killed his mother and her lover and is overwhelmed by the carnage he has created. This was not just a flash of inspiration and Baumberger created a work of similar power for the Vienna Hofburgtheater production of *Medea* in 1917.

The outbreak of war in 1914 dealt a decisive blow to the theatre and as a consequence to the theatre poster. The emphasis even when theatrical productions did happen was on austerity and morale-boosting; light entertainment which had been the strongest stimulant to the artistic theatre poster dwindled. Some interesting theatrical activities and accompanying posters were organized by prisoners of war, but generally serious poster artists were expected to devote their talents to more serious purposes such as entreating men to join up, people to buy war bonds, and other basically propagandist activities.

After the war cultural life recovered quickly, but nothing was ever quite the same again. In general attitudes were split between those who believed a new world order would rise phoenix-like from the ashes to produce a better more humane world to ensure that World War I really had been the 'war to end all wars.' Against this humane liberal ideal were the vestiges of the rabid imperialism which had prompted the war in the first place and which soon spawned the fascist dictatorships of Germany, Italy, and Spain. But in Russia at least the Revolution ensured that this old world order was gone, whatever the shortcomings of what developed in its place.

The theatre reflected the uncertainty and diversity of postwar life while continuing some of the conceptual developments which had been born before the war. A conflict which had always existed to an extent in theatre posters became quite marked. This was that while artists more than ever wished to treat posters as a personal medium of artistic expression, both in themselves and as part of the whole cultural function of the play they were advertising, the dire economic state of postwar Europe meant that the commercial function of the poster as advertisement for a commodity was increasingly important. Naturally in this conflict it was the artistic integrity of the poster and its designer which suffered.

An exception to this rule were those rare productions where the theater de-

signer (especially if he was also the producer) also designed the poster, and again Oskar Kokoschka is the prime example of this as he continued to develop through the 1920s those concepts which he first articulated in the first decade of the century. Expressionist posters were particularly well suited to depicting modern dance, especially dance forms which can be described as forming a part of the Expressionist Movement.

The dancer Mary Wigman is a case in point. Her dance with its Gothic poses and stacatto flourishes is said to have influenced Egon Schiele's conception of the human body and its treatment in the extraordinary portraits he produced. Although Schiele designed one or two posters for exhibitions of his work, he did not design for the theatre. One artist who did design posters for Mary Wigman, however, was the Swiss Laurent F Keller. His poster (page 77) captures what she called her 'absolute' style with a minimum of lines and words.

A stark contrast to the generally frivolous theatre and theatre art which prevailed in Europe and the United States during the 1920s and 1930s is presented by the Soviet Union. During the apocalyptic events of the Revolution and the Civil war posters played a major part in commun-

Below: Vladimir Mayakovsky, Minister of Poetry, encouraged the cultural avant-garde in post-Revolutionary Russia.

Below right: As in the 1890s it was the nightclubs and cabarets of 1920s' Paris which inspired some of the most striking theatre posters.

icating with and mobilising an often illiterate proletariat. This, the shortage of funds and materials, and the need for a direct form of imagery meant that the traditional art form of the *lubok* or woodcut was often employed, an art form which was also popular for its national associations and honest simplicity in inspiring artists of the avant-garde such as Marc Chagall and Mikhail Larionov.

The Russian theatre had been of international importance since before the Revolution with great directors such as Konstantin Stanislavski and Vsevolod Meyerhold. This already existing radicality achieved new vibrancy in the wake of the Revolution, and this is reflected in the design aspects of the theatre, including posters. In the early days of the Soviet Union resources were painfully short and designers had to make do with paintbrushes and plywood, such that this time has been dubbed the 'plywood era.'

The importance that was attached to the theatre may be judged from the prominent artists who were involved in various aspects of theatre design and production. These included Marc Chagall, Nathan Altman, Robert Falk, Isaak Rabinovich, Alexander Rodchenko, Vladimir Mayakovsky, El Lissitzky, and Kasimir Malevich (page 94). One reason for the energy that was devoted to theater design may have been, as El Lissitzky has suggested, that no resources were available for building projects so the creative energy was diverted to theatre design.

For a time, until the early 1920s, stylistic diversity was a feature of the Soviet art scene. Artists as different as Marc Chagall, the dreamy lyricism of his work alluding to aspects of Russian and Jewish

history and culture, could work side by side and collaborate with an artist such as Kasimir Malevich in the forefront of abstraction. In the theatre a specifically Russian form of abstraction, related to Futurism in Italy and Vorticism in Britain, called Constructivism came to dominate theatre design, and art education in general, in the early 1920s.

In theatre-poster design the influence of Constructivism can be seen in the strikingly sparse, often purely typographic designs produced at this time. Of course the continuing paucity of resources is one reason why posters were frequently produced only in black or black and one other color, usually red. The earliest post-Revolutionary posters are the sparsist, typical of which was the playwright Mayakovsky's own design for his play *Mystery Bouffe* of 1918. As time pro-

gressed, pictorial elements were sometimes introduced, such as Yuri Annenkov's poster of 1924 for Alexei Tolstoy's play *The Mutiny of Machines* in which the glorification of machinery alludes to the Union's striving to industrialize to take its place in the modern world.

This poster, and its political subtext, heralded a major change in Soviet theater-poster design and in the whole Soviet art scene generally. While in the early days of the Revolution abstract art had been well and truly hitched to the Bolshevik bandwagon, in 1922 Lenin had published a tract condemning it as decadent and bourgeois. From now on the only acceptable face of Soviet art was to be Socialist Realism, and with the generally more censorious attitude to all cultural activities the Soviet Union lost its place in the avant-garde of world theatre design.

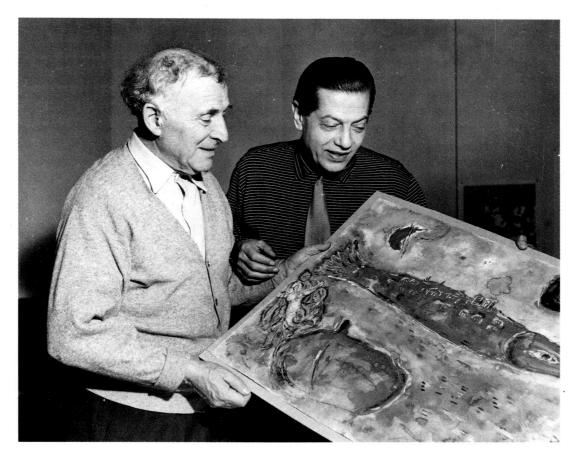

The single most important event for the applied arts, including poster design, in Europe and the United States between the wars was the Exposition de Arts Décoratifs et Industriels Modernes in Paris in 1925. Here was born the concept of Art Deco which influenced all forms of design in the 1920s and 1930s, with its emphasis on the modern, allusions to streamlining and speed, vigour and health, the exotic and the decorative. Art Deco was modern, but it was also fun, an antidote to the gray war years, the epitome of the roaring twenties.

As during that other epoch of daring and glamour, the 1890s, it was Paris which led the way with Art Deco in the 1920s. And it was Paris which produced two of the greatest theater-poster designers of the period in Paul Colin and A M Cassandre. Colin designed all manner of advertising posters, and in the field of entertainment he designed for the music hall, cabarets, including the increasingly popular American Revues Negres, and especially for the Théâtre des Champs Elysées, with whose director Roland de Mare he was friendly. Colin combined the ability to capture the essence of a star's appearance and character in a style influenced by Cubism, with highly readable and avant-garde typography.

Although the cinema was by the 1920s and 1930s making inroads into traditional audiences for popular theatre, the era was as much a golden one for cabaret stars as the 1890s had been. Stars such as the dancer Mistinguett, the singer and dancer Josephine Baker, and Maurice Chevalier enjoyed cult status, an image perpetuated by the poster artists Charles Gesmar, Charles Kiffer, and Jean Carlu; some artists' names were particularly associated with one performer, such as Charles Kiffer with Maurice Chevalier.

The image of carefree, frivolous vitality which this image of the 1920s presents is, of course, only part of the picture. Elsewhere, specifically at the Bauhaus in Germany, designers were addressing themselves to the serious question of designing for the modern age. Their functionalist aesthetic was to be applied to every sort of designed object from whole buildings to cutlery, even painting. Their graphic design, including theater posters, has, as might be anticipated, a sparse, functional quality to it, with the emphasis on typography; it is in many ways the inheritor of Russian Constructivist graphic art. With the rise of Fascism in Germany this type of approach to design became identified with subversion and the theatre of protest, notably different from the cold Neo-Classicism favored by the Nazi establishment.

With the rise of Fascism the organizers of the Bauhaus, such as Walter Gropius and Ludwig Mies van der Rohe, many of whom were Jewish, moved the school to the United States. Perhaps some of their influence can be seen in the workmanlike posters designed under the government's WPA program. During the 1930s' depression the government commissioned many artists and photographers in an effort to mitigate widespread unemployment. The austerity of the period is often reflected in the subdued coloring and restrained typography of the WPA posters.

As with the First War, during World War II the creative energies of poster designers were focussed on morale-boosting and propaganda. The aftermath of the war saw, however, probably greater adjustments of the social order, and more widely dissipated, than had ever been seen before. The map of Europe was redrawn, with the Soviet Empire extending throughout Eastern Europe, and with millions dead or permanently exiled, nothing would ever be quite the same again.

The biggest change affecting the theatre came about through the explosion in electronic media which happened in the 1950s. Soon in affluent societies the majority of homes would have their own television set. Much of the traditional audience for all types of light-entertainment theatre had already defected to the cinema, and many of the rest were now lost to the flickering box in the corner. The effects of this on theatre-poster production might have been disastrous, given the crucial role light entertainment had played in the history of theatre posters.

In fact what happened was that both serious theatre presenting the classical repertoire of Shakespeare, Molière and so on, as well as fringe or art theatre both made increasing use of the poster medium, effectively filling a potential void in production. The other general characteristic of postwar theatre posters which is immediately striking is the extent to which they have become increasingly international in character. There are several reasons for this: partly because of print technology becoming relatively cheaper, theatrical companies traveling extensively, and posters for the same production being used in several different country and more generally because of wider travel among artists including poster artists. Apart from the language of the typography it is hard to tell now the national origins of a theatre poster.

The other single most important influence on poster design generally, and certainly on theatre-poster art, has been

19

the increasingly wide availability of photographic imagery. This is not so much a result of advances in photography itself – the art had been around for more than a century by the 1950s – but in printing technology. Coupled with the relative cost-effectiveness of producing large-size, A3 and above, posters, this has seen no diminution in the production of theatre posters in a period when theatre audiences have been hit by new forms of entertainment.

A style of theatre-poster design which evolved before the war but which has had an enduring appeal ever since is photomontage. Perhaps the century's greatest exponent of this art-form in the poster was the German John Heartfield, who spent many years in the United States before returning to his native land. Together with his brother Wieland Herzfelde he continued the tradition of the Russian Constructivists of the 1920s in using the photomontage technique to express profound cultural and political beliefs.

The brothers became particularly known for posters and stage designs for Brecht plays, for the obvious reason that they expressed the anti-totalitarian ideas and the need for social progress in which they both believed. In 1954 they designed the poster for Brecht's adaptation of Johannes R Becher's *Winter Battle* produced by the Berliner Ensemble. The play centres around the defeat of the German army in Russia in 1941, and the stage design by Karl von Appen was stark to the point of minimalism, with a patch of sky projected above a bare stage, successively gray then white to signify the snow of winter. Heartfield's success consisted in recreating the spirit and something of the appearance of this imagery using photo-

graphy in a way that was as appropriate for the poster medium as von Appen's design was for the stage.

The bleakness of this imagery became a feature of 1950s' theater as the 'theatre of the absurd' of such playwrights as Samuel Beckett came to the fore. Not all theatre of the absurd was, however, as bleak in outlook as Beckett's *Waiting for Godot* and the incongruities of the plays of other playwrights such as Eugene Ionesco were partly responsible for a revival in interest and the use of imagery from Surrealism and Dada which pervaded poster art of all kinds in the 1950s and 1960s.

What distinguishes most theatre posters of the post-war era from those of

before the war is the seriousness of their artistic purpose. As the theatre posters became the preserve of 'serious' or avant-garde theatre it was almost an inevitable consequence that designers of the posters which went with them should wish their work to have an artistic integrity inherent to it. This did not necessarily mean that they were serious – sophisticated, even obscure, humor has often been a feature of theatre posters in our era – but unlike many prewar posters they were rarely a pure and simple adjunct of the show they were promoting.

This is one reason that 'serious' artists were once again attracted to the medium. Sometimes, as with Marc Chagall's 1966

poster for the Metropolitan Opera in New York, the 'art' angle was taken literally and they are merely works of art with typography added as an afterthought. A more significant aspect of this phenomenon was the commissioning of fine artists to design whole dramatic productions, including the poster. David Hockney's designs, once again for the Metropolitan Opera, for a production of Ravel *Parade* are one of the most eminent examples of this, with the poster typography being designed by the artist as an extension of the whole production design. Although it can be seen as a modern-day equivalent of Kokoschka's 'total' designs of half a century earlier, the important difference is that artists such as Hockney are establishment artists designing for an establishment production.

With the 1960s came the era when a light-hearted spirit returned to poster design. Although it was a 'fine art' invention, Pop Art, being inspired by popular imagery – advertising, consumer goods of all kinds – had a natural affinity with such

a popular phenomenon as the poster, and many Pop artists such as Robert Indiana and Robert Rauschenberg designed posters.

After Pop Art, revivalism was the order of the day, with Art Nouveau, especially the work of Beardsley and Mucha, their luxuriance and decadence seeming as appropriate to the 1960s as they had to the 1890s, enjoying a boom. Posters were also an important expression of the decade of protest, with no student bedroom complete without a standard-issue Che Guevara poster. The legitimate theatre responded in a restrained way to the challenge of Pop Art and psychedelia, but it was the shows which sought new audiences which produced the most exuberantly characteristic posters. The poster for the New York musical *Hair* is the psychedelic poster to end all psychedelic posters, and a version of it followed the show across the Atlantic.

Technical wizardry, especially techniques involving photography, have been a major feature of theatre posters since the

1960s. This along with the prevailing taste for pastiche and revivalism might lead one to the conclusion that traditional graphic skills have withered; that this is not so may be seen from many sources, typical of which are the posters of Pole Franciszek Starowieyski. His lyrical yet disturbingly surreal posters with their obviously handrawn lettering belong to a long tradition of poster-making as a craft.

Theatre posters have come a long way in the few hundred years since the first playbills were printed. Until the 1940s they continued to grow in size and technical complexity in keeping with the increasing variety and diversity of dramatic productions. With the advent of television and the continuing growth of the cinema, the theatre as a medium of mass entertainment has lost some of its pulling power. Luckily for us this cannot be said for the theatre poster whose role has changed out of all recognition, from being simply a simple advertising tool to one of the most attractive, accessible, versatile, and international of today's art forms.

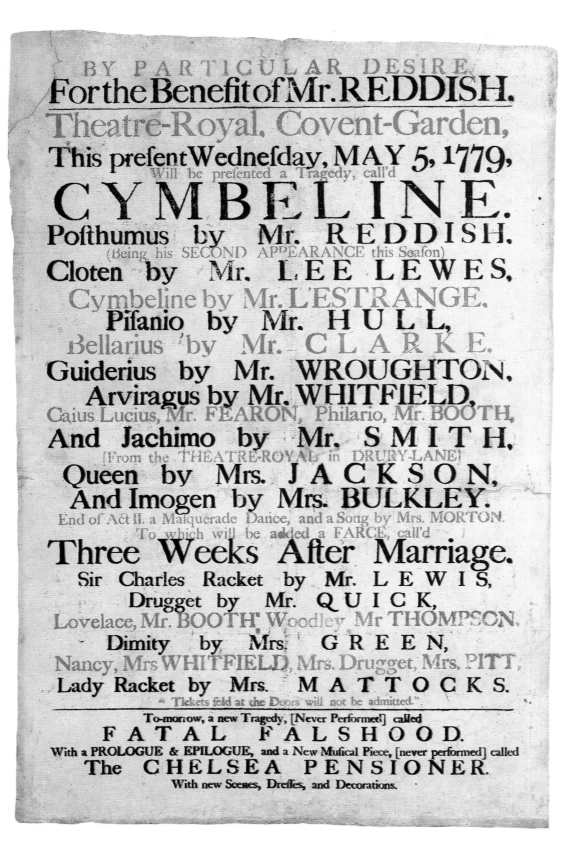

Cymbeline, 1779
Poster for Covent Garden Theatre, London, 5 May 1779
Letterpress
Courtesy of the Trustees of the Victoria and Albert
Museum, London

Siege of Troy, 1833
Poster for Astley's Amphitheatre, London
Woodcut and letterpress
Courtesy of the Trustees of the Victoria and Albert
Museum, London

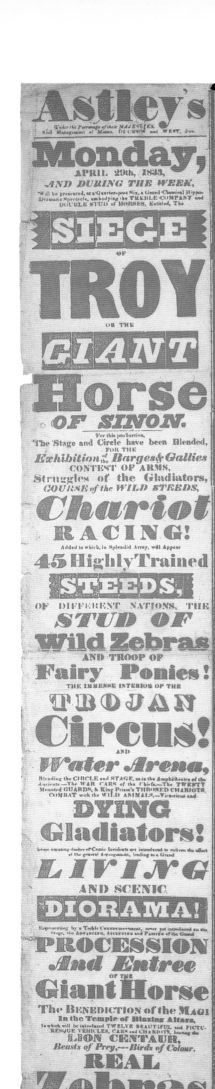

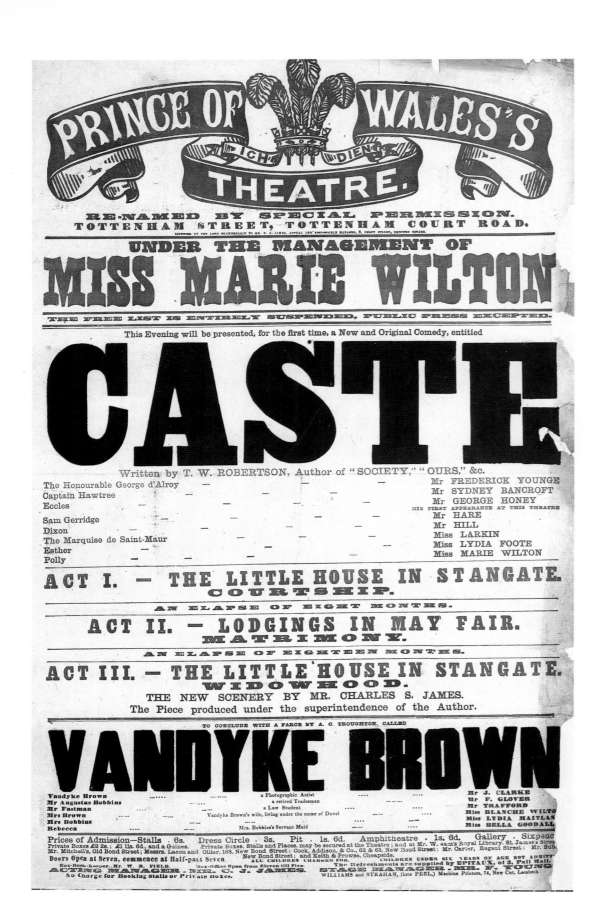

Caste, 1861
Poster for the Prince of Wales's Theatre, London, 6 April 1861
Woodcut and letterpress
Courtesy of the Trustees of the Victoria and Albert
Museum, London

Arrah-na-Pogue, 1865
Poster for the Strand Theatre, London, May 1865
Color lithograph and letterpress
*Courtesy of the Trustees of the Victoria and Albert
Museum, London*

Rubini, c. 1869
Poster for the Egyptian Hall, London
Woodcut and letterpress
Courtesy of the Trustees of the Victoria and Albert Museum, London

Bluebeard, 1871
Poster designed by Matt Morgan for Covent Garden Theatre, London, 26 December 1871
Color lithograph
Courtesy of the Trustees of the Victoria and Albert Museum, London

The Greatest Show on Earth,
1878
Poster for Barnum and Bailey's
Circus
Color lithograph
Private Collection

Iolanthe, 1882
Poster for the Savoy Theatre, London
Color lithograph
Courtesy of the Trustees of the Victoria and Albert
Museum, London

Human Nature, 1885
Poster for Drury Lane Theatre, London, September 1885
Color lithograph
Courtesy of the Trustees of the Victoria and Albert
Museum, London

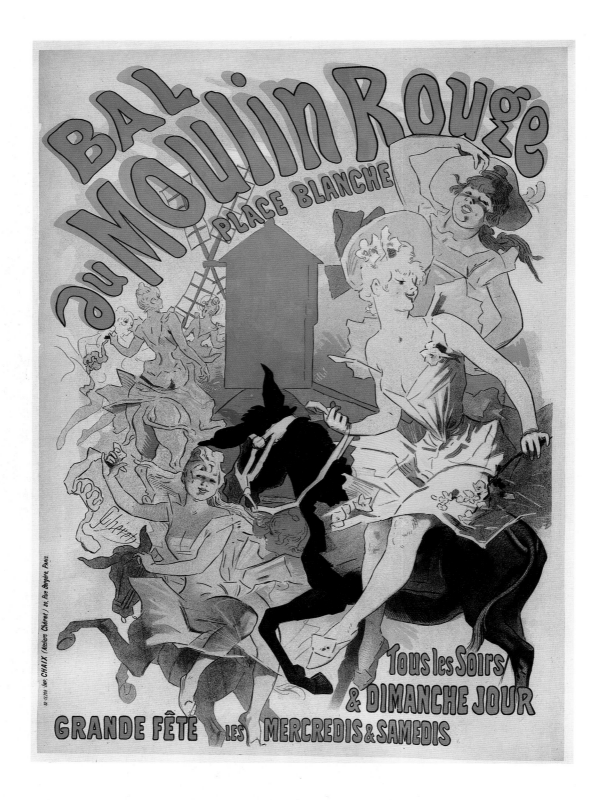

Bal du Moulin Rouge, 1892
Poster designed by Jules Chéret for the Moulin Rouge, Paris
Lithograph in five colors,
48¹³⁄₁₆×35⅝ inches (124×90.5 cm)
Los Angeles County Museum of Art, Dr and Mrs Kurt Wagner

Olympia, 1892
Poster designed by Jules Chéret
Color lithograph
Private Collection

Olympia
anciennes
MONTAGNES RUSSES
Boulevard des Capucines

La Danse du Feu, 1897
Poster designed by Jules Chéret for the Folies-Bergère, Paris
Color lithograph
Private Collection

Loïe Fuller, 1893
Poster designed by Jules Chéret for the Folies-Bergère, Paris
Lithograph in four colors,
43⁵⁄₁₆×32¼ inches (110×81.9 cm)
Los Angeles County Museum of Art, Dr and Mrs Kurt Wagner

Leona Dare, 1891
Poster designed by Jules Chéret
Color lithograph
Private Collection

Alcazar d'Eté Starring Kanjarowa, 1891
Poster designed by Jules Chéret
Color lithograph
Private Collection

Musée Grevin, 1910
Poster designed by Jules Chéret
Lithograph in five colors (before lettering),
47¹/₁₆×32¼ inches (119.5×81.9 cm)
Los Angeles County Museum of Art, Dr and Mrs Kurt Wagner

Le Rêve, 1891
Poster designed by Théophile Steinlen
for the Académie Nationale de Musique
Process print,
34½×25 inches (87.6×63.5 cm)
The Metropolitan Museum of Art, New York,
Mrs Bessie Potter Vonnoh, 1941

Prochainement
Tournée
du
Chat
Noir
avec
Rodolphe Salis
Imp. CHARLES VERNEAU, 114, Rue Oberkampf, PARIS

Moulin Rouge: La Goulue, 1891
Poster designed by Henri de Toulouse-Lautrec
Brush and spatter lithograph in four colors on paper
74½×45 inches (191×115 cm)
Bibliothèque Nationale, Paris

Tournée du Chat Noir, 1896
Poster designed by Théophile Steinlen
Color lithograph
Kunsthalle, Hamburg

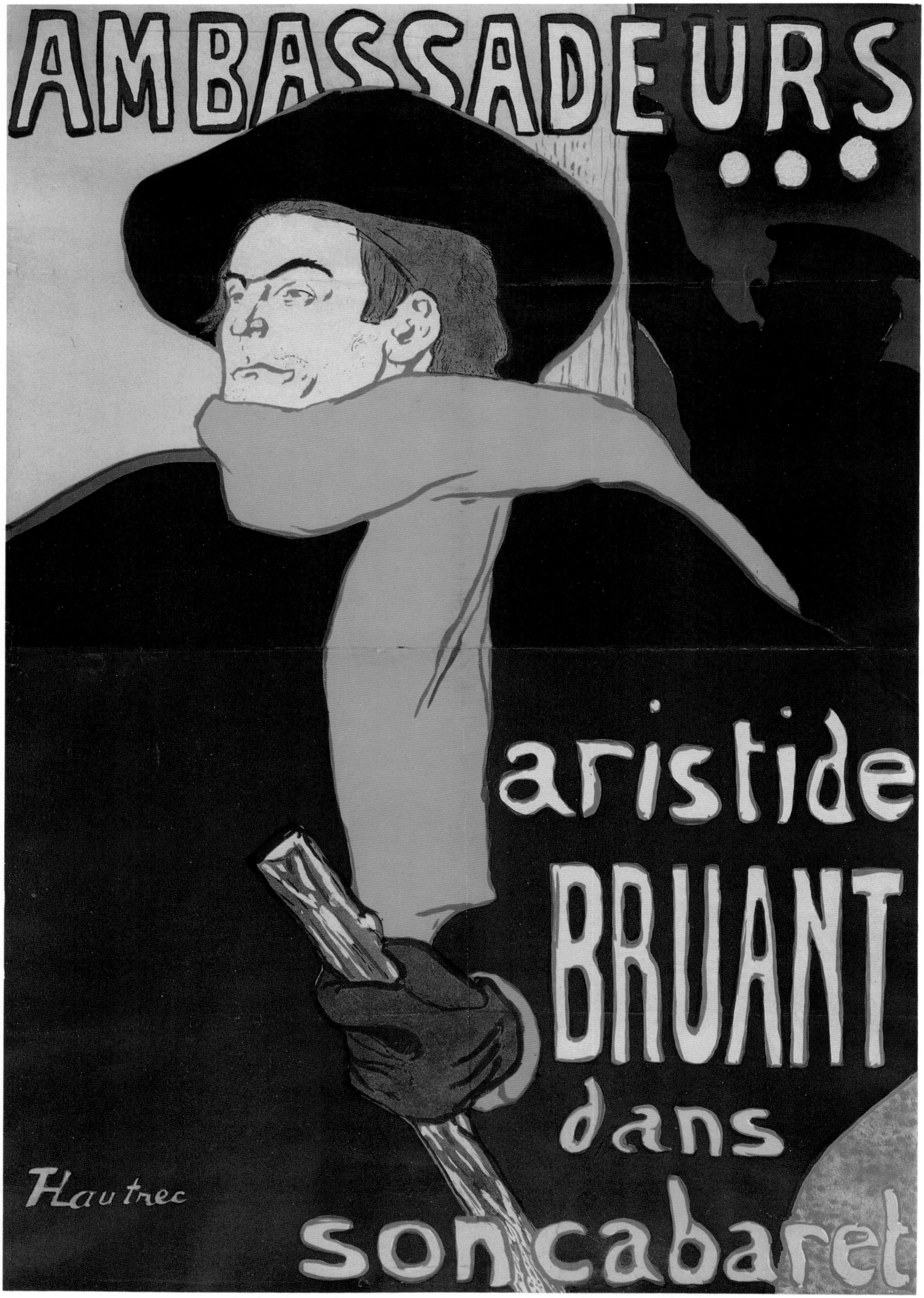
AMBASSADEURS
aristide
BRUANT
dans
son cabaret
HLautrec

Ambassadeurs: Aristide Bruant, 1892
Poster designed by Henri de Toulouse-Lautrec
Brush and spatter lithograph in five colors on paper
53¹⁵⁄₁₆×37⅜ inches (137×95 cm)
San Diego Museum of Art
Gift of the Baldwin M Baldwin Foundation

Aristide Bruant dans son Cabaret, 1893
Poster designed by Henri de Toulouse-Lautrec
Lithograph in four colors,
54½×39 inches (138.4×99 cm)
The Metropolitan Museum of Art, New York
Harris Brisbane Dick Fund, 1932

Jane Avril, 1893
Poster designed by Henri de Toulouse-Lautrec
Lithograph in five colors,
50⅝×37 inches (128.6×94 cm)
The Metropolitan Museum of Art, New York
Harris Brisbane Dick Fund, 1932

Divan Japonais, 1893
Poster designed by Henri de Toulouse-Lautrec
Crayon brush spatter and transferred screen lithograph
30¹⁵⁄₁₆×23⁷⁄₁₆ inches (78.6×59.5 cm)
San Diego Museum of Art
Gift of the Baldwin M Baldwin Collection

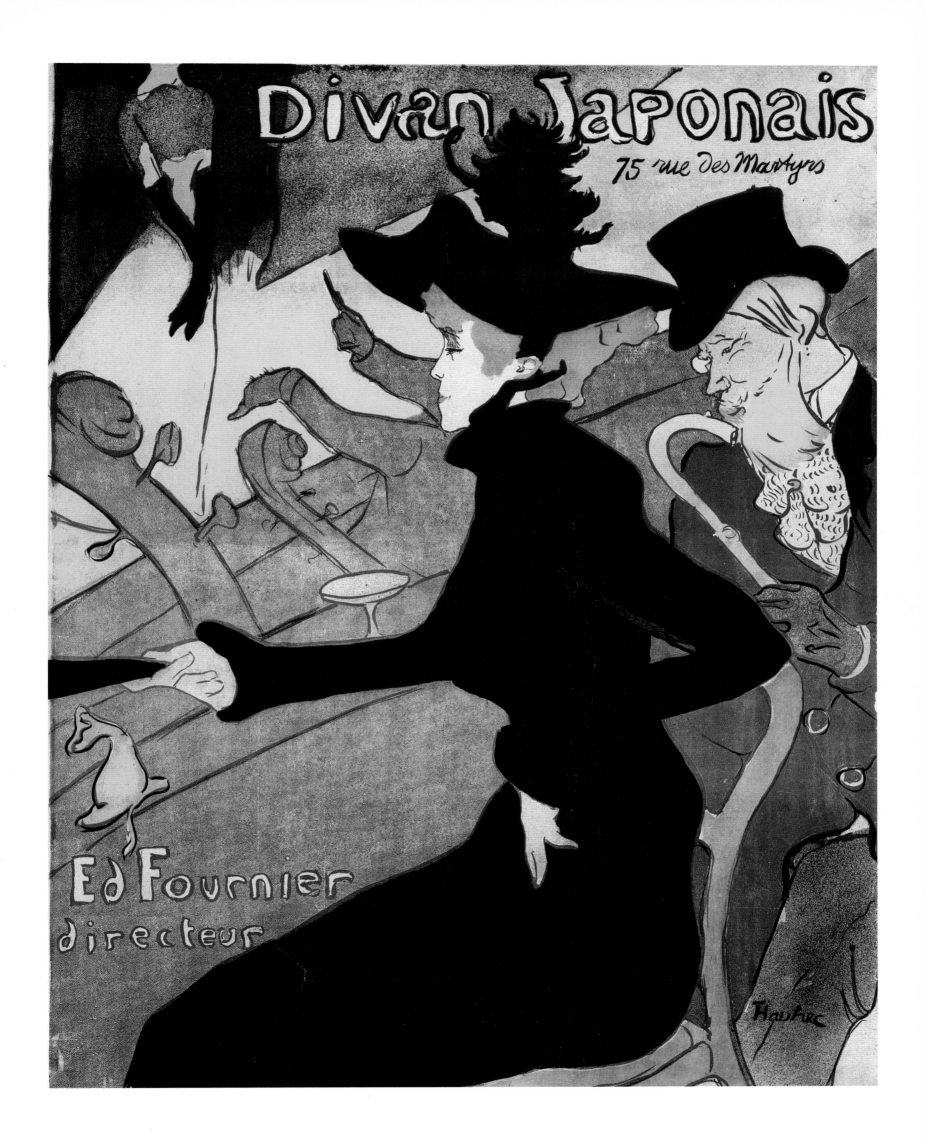

45

May Belfort, 1895
Poster designed by Henri de Toulouse-Lautrec
Color lithograph,
31¼×24¼ inches (87×61.6 cm)
The Metropolitan Museum of Art, New York
Mrs Bessie Potter Vonnoh, 1941

The Troupe of Mlle Eglantine, 1896
Poster designed by Henri de Toulouse-Lautrec
Brush spatter and crayon lithograph in three colors on paper
24½×31½ inches (61.5×77.5 cm)
San Diego Museum of Art
Gift of the Baldwin M Baldwin Foundation

La Dame aux Camélias, 1896
Poster designed by Alphonse Mucha for Sarah
Bernhardt
Lithograph in five colors
Private Collection

Gismonda, 1894-95
Poster designed by Alphonse Mucha for Sarah Bernhardt
Lithograph in five colors
83⅞×29½ inches (213×74.9 cm)
Los Angeles County Museum of Art
Dr and Mrs Kurt Wagner

The Yeoman of the Guard, 1889
Poster designed by Dudley Hardy
for the Savoy Theatre, London
Color lithograph
*Courtesy of the Trustees of the
Victoria and Albert Museum, London*

A Gaiety Girl, c. 1890
Poster designed by Dudley Hardy for Daly's Theatre,
London
Color lithograph
Private Collection

The Only Way (A Tale of Two Cities), 1899
Poster designed by John Hassall
Color lithograph
Courtesy of the Trustees of the Victoria and Albert
Museum, London

A Greek Slave, c. 1899
Poster designed by Stewart Browne for Daly's Theatre,
London/Spa Theatre, Scarborough
Lithograph in five colors
Courtesy of the Trustees of the Victoria and Albert
Museum, London

Dr Nikola, 1902
Poster designed by Stanley L Wood, 1895
Lithograph in three colors
Courtesy of the Trustees of the Victoria and Albert Museum, London

A Comedy of Sighs, 1894
Poster designed by Aubrey Beardsley
for the Avenue Theatre, London
Color lithograph
30×20 inches (76.8×51.2 cm)
Courtesy of the Trustees of the Victoria and Albert Museum, London

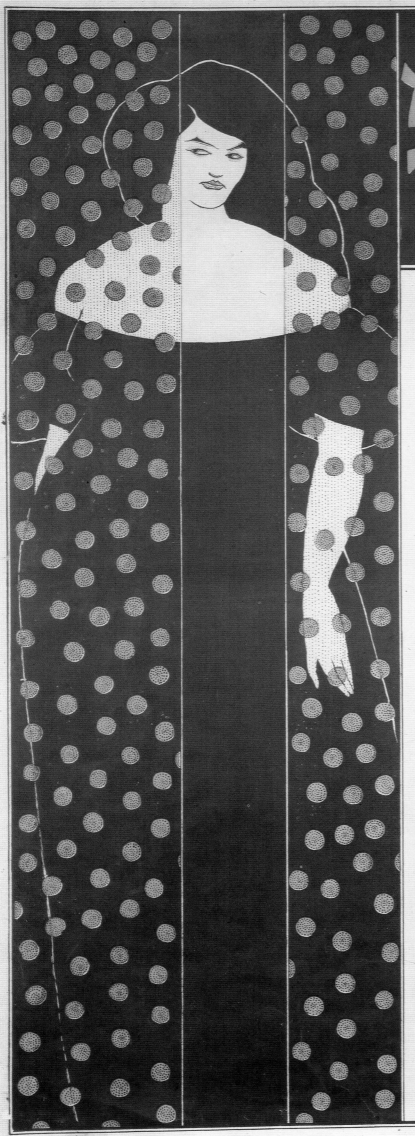

AVENUE THEATRE

(Licensed by the LORD CHAMBERLAIN to GEORGE PAGET, Esq.)

Northumberland Avenue, Charing Cross, W.C.

Manager - Mr. C. T. H. HELMSLEY

ON THURSDAY, March 29th, 1894,

And every Evening at 8-50,

A New and Original Comedy, in Four Acts, entitled,

A COMEDY OF SIGHS!

By JOHN TODHUNTER.

Sir Geoffrey Brandon, Bart.	Mr. BERNARD GOULD
Major Chillingworth	Mr. YORKE STEPHENS
Rev. Horace Greenwell	Mr. JAMES WELCH
Williams	Mr. LANGDON
Lady Brandon (Carmen)	Miss FLORENCE FARR
Mrs. Chillingworth	Miss VANE FEATHERSTON
Lucy Vernon	Miss ENID ERLE

Scene - THE DRAWING-ROOM AT SOUTHWOOD MANOR

Time—THE PRESENT DAY—Late August.

ACT I.	AFTER BREAKFAST
ACT II.	AFTER LUNCH
ACT III.	BEFORE DINNER
ACT IV.	AFTER DINNER

Preceded at Eight o'clock by

A New and Original Play, in One Act, entitled,

The LAND of HEART'S DESIRE

By W. B. YEATS.

Mr. JAS. WELCH. Mr. A. E. W. MASON. & Mr. G. R. FOSS: Miss WINIFRED FRASER. Miss CHARLOTTE MORLAND. & Miss DOROTHY PAGET.

The DRESSES by NATHAN, CLAUDE, LIBERTY & Co., and BENJAMIN. The SCENERY by W. T. HEMSLEY. The FURNITURE by HAMPDEN & SONS.

Stage Manager - Mr. G. R. FOSS

Doors open at 7-40, Commence at 8. Carriages at 11.

PRICES:--Private Boxes, £1 1s. to £4 4s. Stalls, 10s.6d. Balcony Stalls. 7s. Dress Circle. 5s. Upper Circle (Reserved), 3s. Pit, 2s.6d. Gallery, 1s.

On and after March 26th, the Box Office will be open Daily from 10 to 5 o'clock, and 8 till 10. Seats can be Booked by Letter, Telegram, or Telephone No. 35297.

NO FEES.　　　NO FEES.　　　NO FEES.

STAFFORD & CO. NETHERFIELD, NOTTINGHAM.

Cinderella, 1895
Poster designed by the
Beggarstaff Brothers for the
Drury Lane Theatre, London
Lithograph in three colors
Kunsthalle, Hamburg

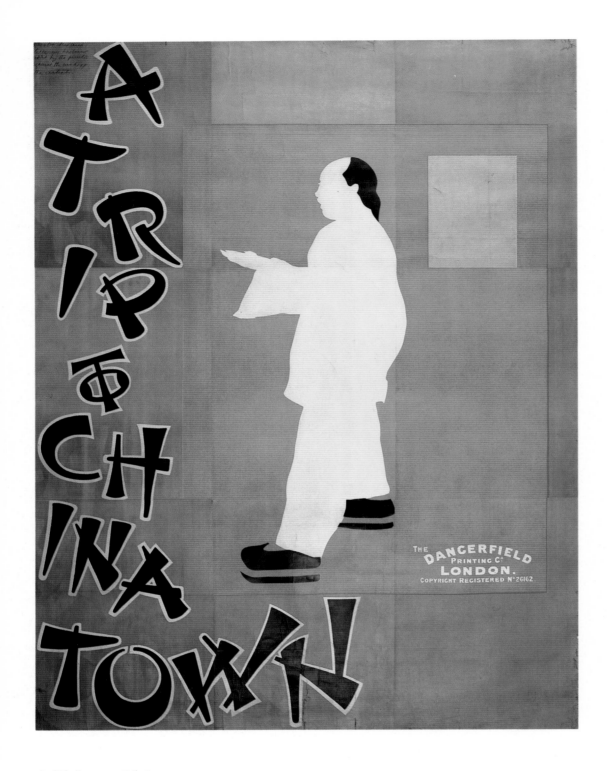

A Trip to Chinatown, 1895
Poster designed by the Beggarstaff Brothers
Lithograph in three colors
Kunsthalle, Hamburg

Daly's Theatre, c. 1900
Poster designed by Edgar Wilson
Lithograph in four colors
Private Collection

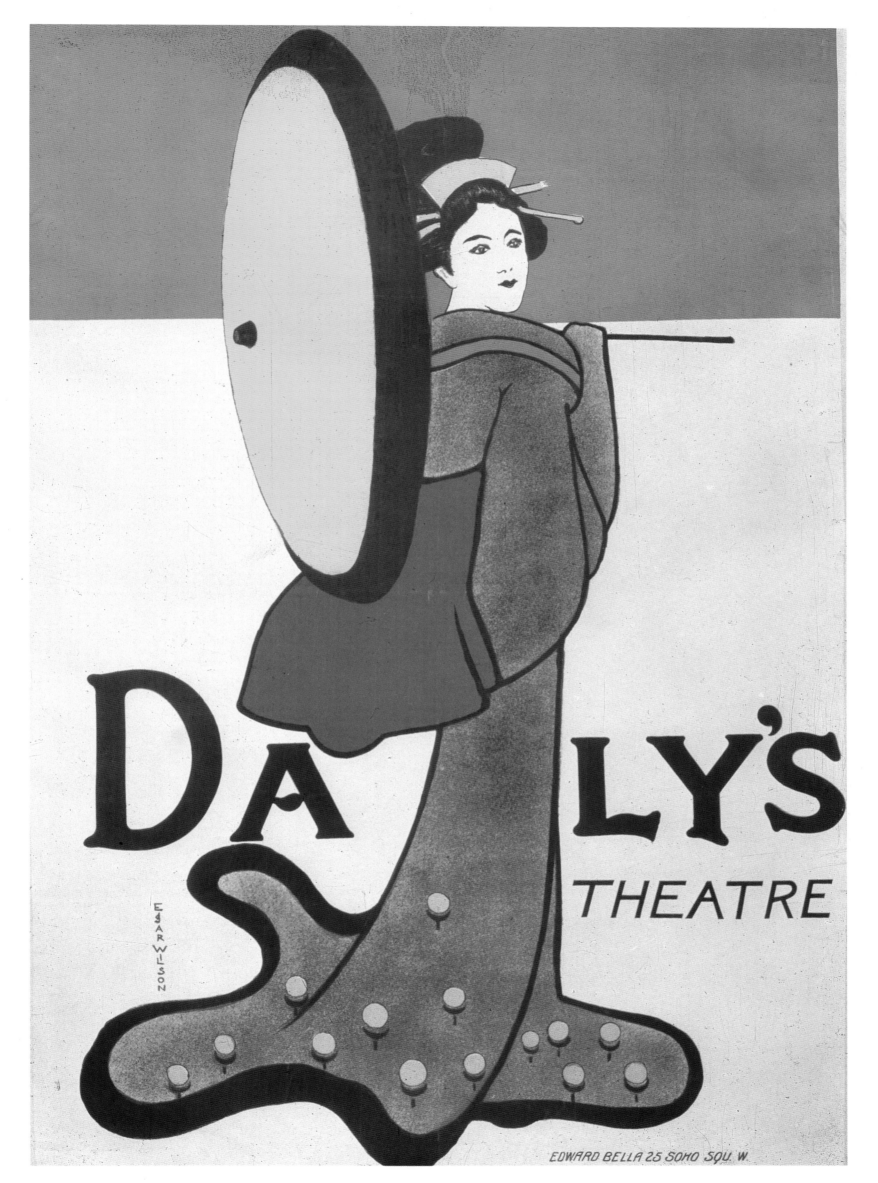

DALY'S
THEATRE

E&AR WILSON

EDWARD BELLA 25 SOHO SQU. W.

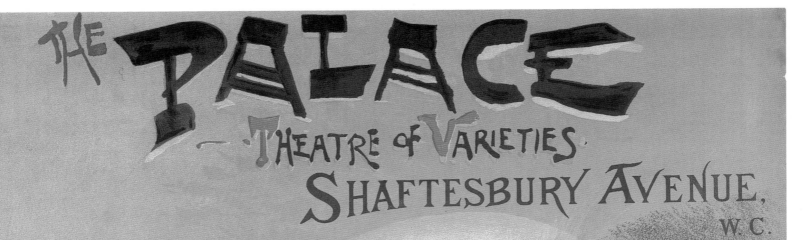

THE PALACE

—THEATRE of VARIETIES·

SHAFTESBURY AVENUE,
W.C.

Every
Evening
LES

MINSTRELS

PARISIENS

Manager,
MR. CHARLES MORTON.

Loïe Fuller, c. 1900
Poster designed by Pal
Lithograph in four colors
48×33 inches (121.9×83.8 inches)
*Los Angeles County Museum of Art,
Dr and Mrs Kurt Wagner*

Les Minstrels Parisiens, 1895
Poster designed by Pal (Jean Paleologu)
Lithograph in four colors
*Courtesy of the Trustees of the Victoria and Albert
Museum, London*

Concert de la Pepinière, 1902
Poster designed by Jules-Alexandre Grun
Lithograph in four colors
Private Collection

Jane d'Alma, 1904
Poster designed by Adrien Barrère
Lithograph in four colors
Private Collection

La Revue des Folies-Bergère, c. 1905
Poster designed by Adrien Barrère
Lithograph in six colors
Private Collection

Frühlingserwachen, 1903
Poster designed by Edmund Edel for the Berlintheater
Lithograph in four colors
Kunstgewerbemuseum, Zurich

Pietà, 1908
Poster designed by Oskar Kokoschka
Color lithograph
Osterreichisches Museum für Angewandte Kunst, Vienna

Prinz Goldhaar und die Gänzehirtin, 1909
Poster designed by Willy F Burger
Lithograph in three colors
Kunstgewerbemuseum, Zurich

Koenig Oedipus, 1911
Poster designed by Ernst Stern
Lithograph in three colors
Kunstgewerbemuseum, Zurich

Bernerstadttheater, 1911
Poster designed by Ernst Linck
Lithograph in three colors
Kunstgewerbemuseum, Zurich

Parsifal, 1913
Poster designed by Ernst Georg Ruegg
Lithograph in three colors
Kunstgewerbemuseum, Zurich

Stadttheater Zürich

Parsifal

Ein Bühnenweihfestspiel
von Richard Wagner

<u>Sechs Aufführungen 1913</u>

| Sonntag 31. August | Freitag 5. September | Dienstag 9. September |
| Mittwoch 3. September | Sonntag 7. September | Donnerstag 11. September |

Billettbestellungen können an die Kasse des Stadttheaters und an das
Reisebureau von Alfr. Kuoni, Zürich, Bahnhofplatz. 7 gerichtet werden

Kunstanstalt J. C. Müller, Zürich 8

Theaterkunst Ausstellung, 1914
Poster designed by Carl Roesch
Lithograph in four colors
Kunstgewerbemuseum, Zurich

Otake, 1914, 1925
Poster designed by Paul Leni
Lithograph in three colors
Kunstgewerbemuseum, Zurich

74

Orchester Olah, 1915
Poster designed by Otto Baumberger
Lithograph in two colors
Kunstgewerbermuseum, Zurich

Maskenball, 1914
Poster designed by Paul Scheurich
Lithograph in three colors
Kunstgewerbemuseum, Zurich

Die Wilden Schwäne, 1916
Poster designed by Burkhard Mangold
Lithograph in two colors
Kunstgewerbemuseum, Zurich

Mary Wigman, 1919
Poster designed by Laurent F Keller
Lithograph in two colors
Kunstgewerbemuseum, Zurich

Le Roi David, 1921
Poster designed by Jean Morax
Lithograph in four colors
Kunstgewerbermuseum, Zurich

Théâtre de la Chauve-Souris, 1921
Program cover designed by N Remisoff
Lithograph in seven colors
*Courtesy of the Trustees of the Victoria and Albert
Museum, London*

THÉATRE DE LA CHAUVE-SOURIS

N.REMISOFF.

Cinquième Programme

The Bluebird, 1909
Playbill design by Frederick Cayley Robinson
Watercolor, pen and ink, and pencil
Haymarket Theatre, London

Macbeth, 1911
Poster designed by Edmund Dulac
Lithograph in three colors
Courtesy of the Trustees of the Victoria and Albert
Museum, London

Shakespeare's **Macbeth**
His Majesty's Theatre

MILES. LITHO. LONDON w.

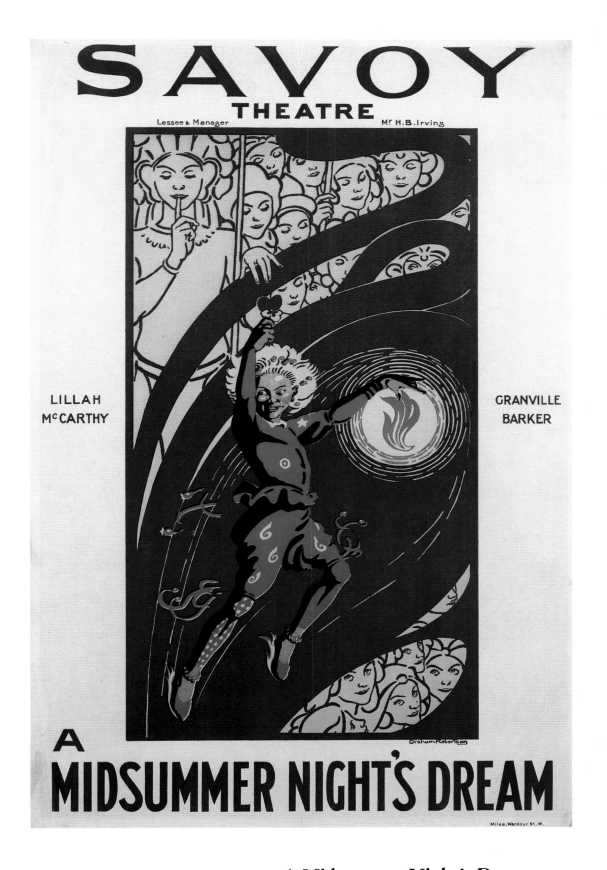

A Midsummer Night's Dream, 1914
Poster designed by Graham Robertson
for the Savoy Theatre, London
Lithograph in three colors
*Courtesy of the Trustees of the Victoria and Albert
Museum, London*

Eightpence a Mile, 1913
Poster designed by G K Benda
for the Alhambra Theatre, London
Lithograph in four colors
*Courtesy of the Trustees of the
Victoria and Albert Museum, London*

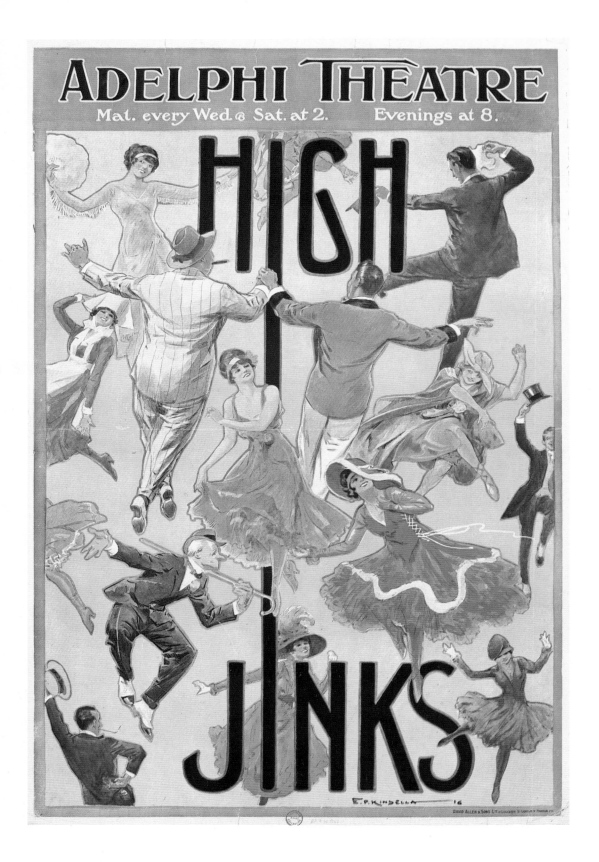

High Jinks, 1916
Poster designed by E P Kindella for the Adelphi Theatre,
London
Color lithograph
*Courtesy of the Trustees of the Victoria and Albert
Museum, London*

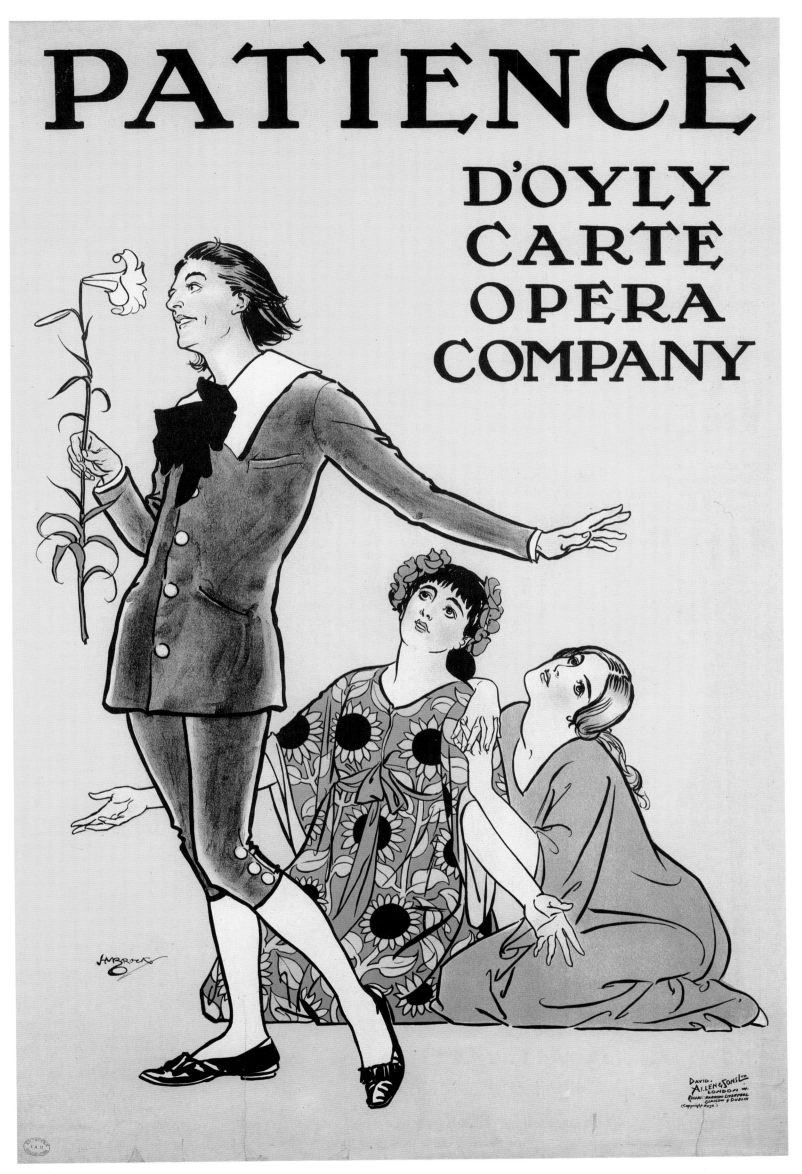

Jumble Sale, c. 1920
Poster designed by G K Benda
Lithograph in two colors
*Courtesy of the Trustees of the Victoria and Albert
Museum, London*

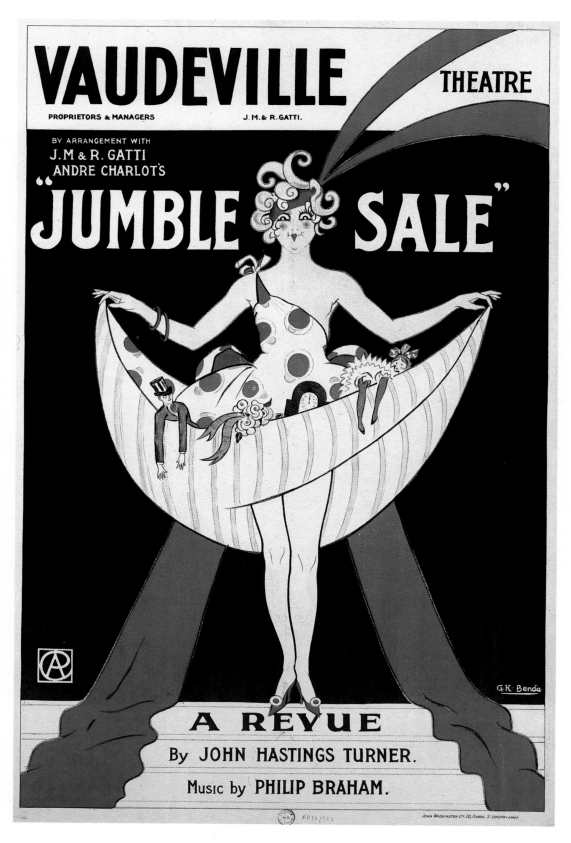

THE BEGGAR'S OPERA

By Mr Gay.

C. LOVAT FRASER, 1920.

LYRIC THEATRE HAMMERSMITH.

The Glass Slipper, 1925
Poster designed by Alexander Calder
for the Guild Theatre
Lithograph in four colors
The New York Public Library at Lincoln Center

Karsavina in *Le Spectre de la Rose,* c. 1923
Poster designed by Jean Cocteau for the Ballets Russes
Lithograph in three colors
The Fine Art Society, London

Pulcinella, 1923
Program cover featuring set designed by Pablo Picasso
Color lithograph
Courtesy of the Trustees of the Victoria and Albert
Museum, London

Ballets Russes de Diaghilev, 1939
Poster designed by Pablo Picasso
Color lithograph,
23⅝×15¾ inches (60×40 cm)
Private Collection

BALLETS RUSSES
DE DIAGHILEW
1909 - 1929

MARS - AVRIL 1939

MUSÉE DES ARTS DÉCORATIFS
Palais du Louvre _ Pavillon de Marsan , 107, rue de Rivoli

ENTRÉE 6 FRANCS

Barbette, c. 1925
Poster designed by Paul Colin
Gouache and pencil
Bibliothèque de l'Opéra, Paris

Les Billy Arnolds, 1925
Poster designed by Paul Colin
Gouache and pencil
Bibliothèque de l'Opéra, Paris

A Christmas Carol c. 1935
WPA poster for the Federal Theatre for Youth,
Cleveland, Ohio
Lithograph in three colors
George Mason University

Dr Mabuso, c. 1922
Poster designed by Kasimir Malevich
Lithograph in three colors
Tretyakov Museum, Moscow

Night Must Fall, c. 1935
WPA poster for the Alcazar Theatre, Federal Theatre Project
Lithograph in three colors
George Mason University

Flight c. 1935
WPA poster for the Federal Theatre Project
Lithograph in four colors
George Mason University

FLIGHT

BY OSCAR SAUL AND LOU LANTZ · PRESENTED BY
THEATRE FOR YOUTH · W.P.A. FEDERAL THEATRE PROJECT

HECKSCHER THEATRE
1 EAST 104th STREET
THURS. AND FRI. AT 4:00 PM · SAT. 2:30 & 8:30 PM

FEDERAL ART PROJECT

N.Y.C.

FEDERAL DANCE THEATRE
PRESENTS

SALUT AU MONDE

ADAPTED FROM A POEM OF THAT NAME
BY WALT WHITMAN

CHOREOGRAPHY AND
DIRECTION BY TAMIRIS
MUSIC COMPOSED BY
GENEVIEVE PITOT
COSTUMES DESIGNED
BY ROBERT BYRNE
DON OSCAR BECQUE
MANAGING PRODUCER

FEDERAL ART PROJECT

The Ivory Door, 1938-39
WPA poster for the Federal Theatre for Youth,
Cleveland, Ohio
Lithograph in three colors
George Mason University

Salut au Monde, 1936
WPA Poster for the Federal Dance Theatre
Lithograph in four colors
George Mason University

DIE MUTTER

von Brecht nach Motiven aus Gorkis Roman · Musik von Hanns Eisler

BERLINER
ENSEMBLE

Ausstattung
Caspar Neher

Gemalte Projektion
Hainer Hill

Film- u. Fotoprojektion
Heartfield Herzfelde

Musikalische Leitung
Adolf Guhl

Mitwirkende
Helene Weigel
Ernst Busch
Carola Braunbock
Herta Eckert
Annemarie Hase
Angelika Hurwicz
Jeanne Kiefer
Margarete Körting
Betty Loewen
Regine Lutz
Ilse Nürnberg
Käthe Reichel
Hanna Rieger
Sabine Thalbach
Bella Waldritter
Eleonore Zetzsche
Johannes Bergfeldt
Gerhard Bienert
Arthur Christoph
Hans Eckert
Friedrich Gnass
Erwin Geschonneck
Harry Gillmann
Willi Hübner
Ernst Kahler
Wolf Kaiser
Peter Kalisch
Alfred Land
Peter Lehmbrock
Rudolf Lucas
Wladimir Marfiak
Erich Nadler
Joseph Noerden
Georg Peter-Pilz
Werner Pledath
Gert Schaefer
Heinz Schubert
Willi Schwabe
Kurt Soefern
Kurt Sperling
Wolfgang E. Struck
Adolf Tamke
Heino Thalbach
Axel Triebel u. a.

PHOTO: WALTER WERK

BRÜDER HEARTFIELD HERZFELDE

M 401

Druck: VEB Deutsche Graphische Werkstätten, Leipzig.

3/500
20. 2. 51

Die Mutter, 1951
Poster designed by John Heartfield
Color photolithograph
Kunsthalle, Hamburg

Das Glockenspiel des Kreml, 1952
Poster designed by John Heartfield
Color photolithograph
Kunsthalle, Hamburg

Theatre Programs, 1945-
Various designers and printing processes
Courtesy of the Trustees of the Victoria and Albert
Museum, London

Godspell, c. 1970
Color lithograph
21⅜×13½ inches (54.3×34.3 cm)
Private Collection

The New National Theatre is Yours, 1976
Poster designed by Tom Phillips
Color lithograph
Courtesy of the Trustees of the Victoria and Albert
Museum, London

Grand Revue, c. 1970
Poster designed by Tadanori Yokoo
Photolithograph in eight colors
Private Collection

Nederlander Productions, Inc., The Shubert Organization
and the John F. Kennedy Center for The Performing Arts
in association with Theatre Now, Inc.
present

Zero Mostel
in
Fiddler on the Roof
A MUSICAL

Book by JOSEPH STEIN
(Based on Sholom Aleichem's stories by special permisson of Arnold Perl)

Music by JERRY BOCK

Lyrics by SHELDON HARNICK

Direction Reproduced by   Choreography Reproduced by
RUTH MITCHELL   TOMMY ABBOTT

Original Direction & Choreography by
JEROME ROBBINS

Settings by   Costumes by   Lighting by
BORIS ARONSON   PATRICIA ZIPPRODT   KEN BILLINGTON

Orchestrations by   Vocal Arrangements by   Dance Music Arranged by
DON WALKER   MILTON GREENE   BETTY WALBERG

Originally Produced by HAROLD PRINCE

Fiddler on the Roof, c. 1974
Color lithograph
22×14 inches (55.9×35.6 cm)
Private Collection

The Rocky Horror Show, c. 1980
Color lithograph
22×14 inches (55.9×35.6 cm)
Private Collection

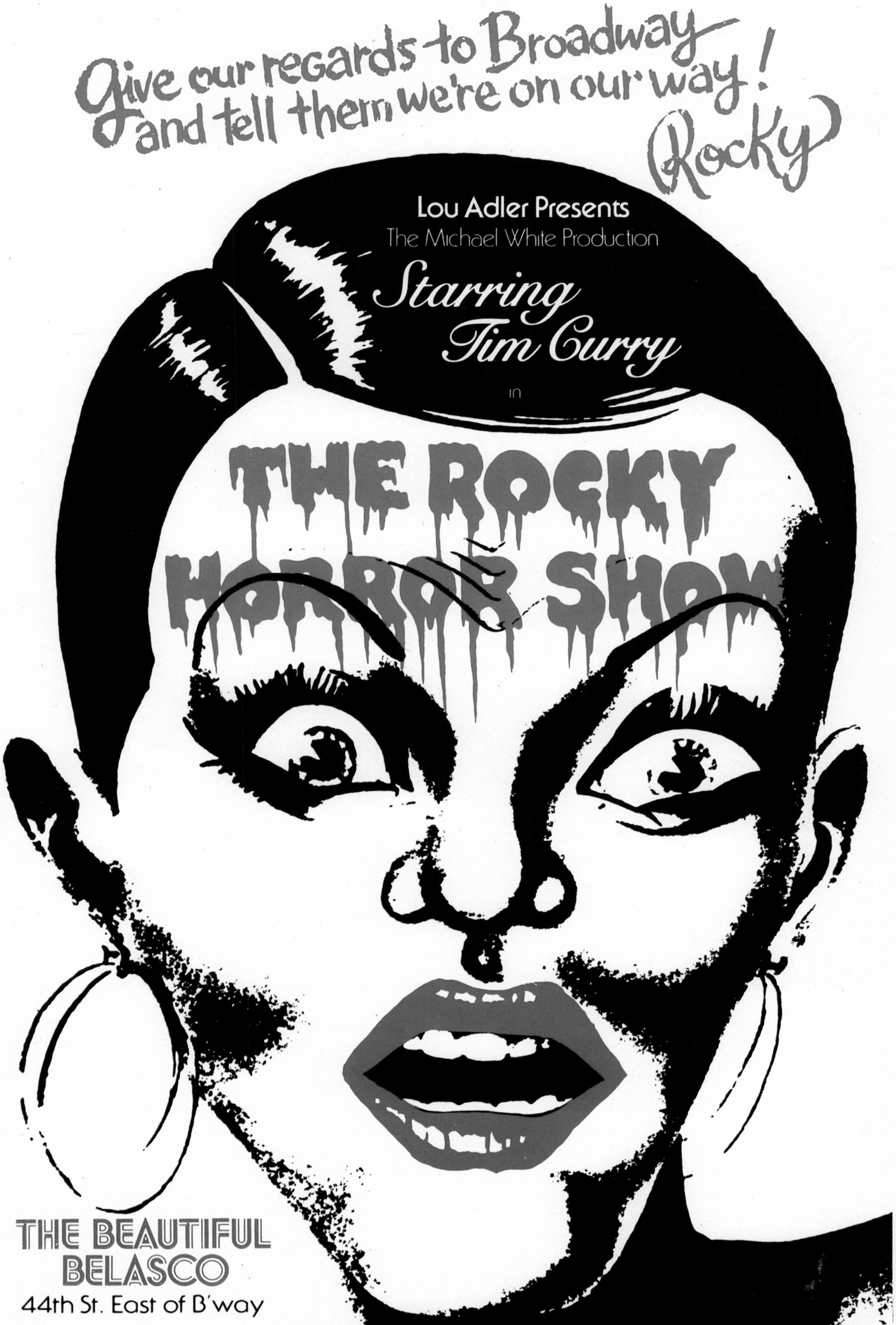

give our regards to Broadway and tell them we're on our way!
Rocky
Lou Adler Presents
The Michael White Production
Starring
Tim Curry
in
THE ROCKY HORROR SHOW
THE BEAUTIFUL BELASCO
44th St. East of B'way

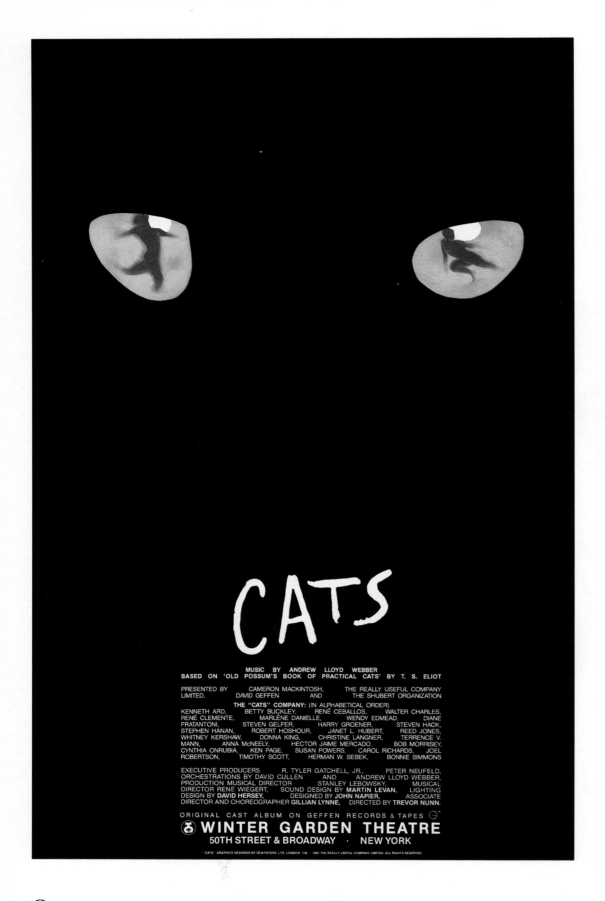

Cats, 1981
Poster designed by Dewynters Plc
© TM 1981 The Really Useful Group Limited
Photolithograph
22×13⅞ inches (55.9×35.3 cm)
Private Collection

Les Misérables, 1990
Photolithograph Poster for Cameron Mackintosh
22×14 inches (55.9×35.6 cm)
Private Collection

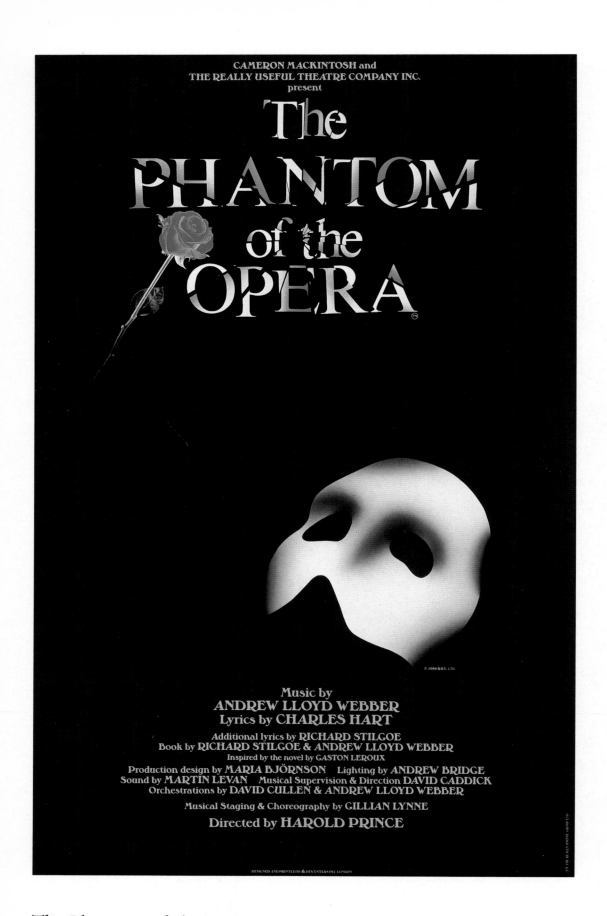

The Phantom of the Opera, 1986
Poster designed by Dewynters plc
© TM 1986 The Really Useful Group Limited
Photolithograph
22×13⅞ inches (55.9×35.6 cm)
Private Collection

Miss Saigon, 1988
Poster designed by Dewynters Plc
for Cameron Mackintosh
Photolithograph
22×13⅞ inches (55.9×35.3 cm)
Private Collection

CAMERON MACKINTOSH
presents

JONATHAN PRYCE
LEA SALONGA

HINTON BATTLE   WILLY FALK
LIZ CALLAWAY   BARRY K. BERNAL
At certain performances
KAM CHENG
plays the role of 'Kim'
in

Music by
CLAUDE-MICHEL SCHÖNBERG
Lyrics by
RICHARD MALTBY, JR.
& ALAIN BOUBLIL
Adapted from original French lyrics by
ALAIN BOUBLIL
Additional material
RICHARD MALTBY, JR.
Musical supervision
DAVID CADDICK & ROBERT BILLIG
Orchestrations by
WILLIAM D. BROHN

Directed by
NICHOLAS HYTNER
Musical staging by
BOB AVIAN
Production designed by
JOHN NAPIER
Costumes designed by
ANDREANE NEOFITOU
& SUZY BENZINGER
Lighting by
DAVID HERSEY
Sound by
ANDREW BRUCE

A MUSICAL
BY ALAIN BOUBLIL AND
CLAUDE-MICHEL SCHÖNBERG

⊕ BROADWAY THEATRE
BROADWAY & 53RD STREET
ORIGINAL LONDON CAST RECORDING AVAILABLE ON GEFFEN RECORDS ⊖

111

Acknowledgments

The publisher would like to thank Martin Bristow who designed this book and Elizabeth Montgomery who did the picture research. We would also like to thank the following agencies, individuals, and institutions for supplying the illustrations:

Archiv für Kunst und Geschichte, Berlin: 18 (above left)
The Bettman Archive: pages 6, 7 (both), 9 (above right and below left), 10 (above), 13 (above), 15, 16 (below), 17
Bibliothèque Nationale, Paris: page 11 (below), 12 (both above), 13 (below), 41
Bibliothèque de l'Opéra, Paris: pages 92, 93
Bridgeman Art Library: page 14
British Film Institute, London: page 20 (below)
Camera Press: page 20 (above)
René Dazy, Paris: page 18 (below)
The Fine Art Society, London/Bridgeman Art Library: page 89
George Mason University: pages 96, 97, 98, 99
Haymarket Theatre, London/Bridgeman Art Library: page 80
Kunstgewerbemuseum, Zurich: 66, 68, 69, 70, 71, 72, 73, 74, 75, 76, 77, 78
Kunsthalle, Hamburg: page 40, 56-57, 58, 100, 101

Los Angeles County Museum of Art, Dr and Mrs Kurt Wagner: pages 32, 34, 38, 49, 61
The Metropolitan Museum of Art, New York: page 12 (below; Rogers Fund, 1922), 39, 46 (Mrs Bessie Potter Vonnoh, 1941), 43 (Harris Brisbane Dick Fund, 1932), 44
The New York Public Library at Lincoln Center: page 88
Osterreichisches Museum für Angewandte Kunst: 67
Private Collection: page 10 (below), 103, 104, 106, 107, 108 (© The Really Useful Group Ltd), 109, 110 (© The Really Useful Group Ltd), 111
Private Collection/Bridgeman Art Library: pages 28-29, 33, 35, 36, 37, 48, 51, 59, 62, 63, 65-65, 87, 91
Rijksmuseum, Amsterdam: page 16 (above)
Roger-Viollet, Paris: page 19
San Diego Museum of Art, Gift of the Baldwin M Baldwin Foundation: page 42, 45, 47
Sutcliffe Gallery, Whitby: page 8 (by agreement with the Whitby Literay and Philosophical Society)
Tretyakov Museum, Moscow/Bridgeman Art Library: page 94
Courtesy of the Trustees of the Victoria and Albert Museum, London: pages 2, 9 (below right), 11 (above), 22, 23, 24, 25, 26, 27, 30, 31, 50, 52, 53, 54, 55, 60, 79, 81, 82, 83, 84, 85, 86, 90, 102, 105
Vintage Magazine Company: page 21